Material Matters

Material Matters

Poems by

Tom Holmes

Cover art:
https://commons.wikimedia.org/wiki/File:Flammarion.jpg.
Public Domain
Ⓔ

Cover design: Shay Culligan

ISBN: 978-1-952326-34-9

Kelsay Books
502 South 1040 East, A-119
American Fork, Utah, 84003

"When I have made a sentence out of something, what has that something to do with the sentence?"
— Thomas Mann

Acknowledgments

These poems or versions of the poems first appeared in these journals:

Alabama Literary Review: "Dream Atlas" (formerly "The Museum of Dreams")

The American Journal of Poetry: "The First Line of Prayer," "Guide to Medieval Reading"

Beechwood Review: "Scripture"

Birmingham Poetry Review: "The Orange Movement and the Rise and Fall of *Orange Nucléaire*"

Bitter Oleander: "The Cartographer's Credo," "Transcendental Homelessness" (formerly "The Waftiness of Transcendental Homelessness")

Blue Lyra Review: "Arctic Circle Cautioning (352 B.C.)"

Carbon Culture Review: "1439 — This Is How the Middle Ages End"

Clementine Poetry Journal: "The World from a Genoese"

Diaphanous: "Under the Spell of an Increasingly Deadly Vowel Movement"

Dirty Chai: "The Mapmaker's Drawing in Time"

The Homestead Review: "The Treasure Gaze as Explained by Abraham Cresques Using His Catalan Atlas"

The Indianola Review: "Deconstruction"

Lost River Literary Magazine: "The Unmentionable Places for the Carographer," "Sometimes I Contact My First Love Late at Night"

Lyre Lyre: "Political Spin (A Turn in History)"

The Meadow: "Hic Sunt Vaccas"

Modern Poetry Quarterly Review: "Lesson Plan: Teaching Terroir 1638 A.D."

Of/with: "The White Space"

Product: "Drawing to Scale (900 A.D.)"

Roanoke Review: "Sometimes the Night Arrives Without Design"

Route 7 Review: "The Museum of Cartography"

Sheepshead Review: "Even Now"

Sugar House Review: "In Bas-Relief" (formerly "Anna Beth Rowe in Bas-Relief"), "Johannes Deville, the First Atheist Cartographer" (formerly "Johannes Deville's Shadow"), "Still the Bells"

Suisun Valley Review: "The Vertical Moment"

The Tishman Review: "Conversation on the Balcony"

Xavier Review: "Exile on Longleaf Trace"

you are here: the journal of creative geography: "Martin Behaim to Pope Clement VI on the Incomplete Maps (1342 A.D.)"

"The Mapmaker's Drawing in Time" was nominated for Best of the Net.

Contents

III

I

In Bas-Relief

You said you found a city once in lights,
with shadows worn into the roads and walls.
You said you saw no people nor no names
on street signs, and the city felt erased.
At city hall, you trembled at the door.
You said you feared a history of ghosts,
or worse, no recorded history at all.
You wrestled with the door, then found an in.
Behind the entrance desk you saw, you said,
the city on the wall in full relief.
The rivers colored blue, the streets in pink.
You traced where you had been and still to go.
You wrote on it what you would later say
and transcribed the city with where you'd been.

The Mapmaker's Drawing in Time

Sometimes I steady my hand over Europe
and Asia Minor and recreate the Dark Ages.
Sometimes I press my palm on the wet ink
boundaries and press it to my other palm,
then cup my ears and listen to the prayers
of believers in churches and mosques
before executions, of mothers burned
in purple and pink hijabs, and kosher
grocery store shoppers before they're shot.
I'd wash my hands of that but it's like erasing
a country or lands from the world. I press
instead my hands together and ask
of Abraham to re-present the facts
before him to be known and not believed.
Sometimes I draw a boundless world.

Political Spin (a Turn in History)

Even before I read about Archimedes,
the world spun round the sun
and there were wars.
                    He was contracted
to trace the origins of it all,
so he inscribed his name on vellum
and spoke the oath. He etched the world
on copperplate for permanence,
curled it to a sphere, and rolled it out.
He impressed in the floor's tapestry
an oblong figure-eight path. He said,
the earth cuts through space like this.
Perfection, he proved, has no beginning,
is beginning always.
                    The Romans,
even now in this history
book, roll away his world straight
to Rome in spring. It cracks
like an egg. It's empty except for proofs
of revolution. In that half, they stir
a fire. In the other, they brand their gods.

Dedication from *Love's Apostrophe*, an Anonymous Book of Love Poems from 1082 A.D.

The pigments and papers smell fresh, a sign
of authenticity, and I am privileged
to own this library and all its words
transcribed from learnéd men to work through.
I assume the thoughts are true, not figments
from tired copy boys. No matter, I
read them to recollect the words I need,
when you are gone, to serenade your return.
I wrote this book of lyrics with my hand
and stylus. No copyist's instrument
interrupted my lines. You can trace
then where I have been. Each line is direct.
In case you know not the value of words,
each poem's initial letter is pressed with gold.

Dream Atlas

The Smartest Person in the World

They say her hairs are antennas. She's always receiving
and quiet. When she's near, I don't know if I'm talking
to you or if she is speaking through us. They say
when she dies, she travels back in time and invents language.
She's died many times. I don't know what I'm saying.

Cathedral

The forest sways with 50-foot high toothbrushes.
Each morning, the sky bleeds. The bristles drip
long beady strings all day. At night, the dryness
arrives with fallen-egg-stenched winds shredding
through bristles like songs through cracked ceramic teeth.

Judgment Day and the Undermining

The cave is filled with cops. They are freeing
their prosthetic hats and batons. They are mixing
tickets with melted coins. They are smearing
it across the walls and floors. They are alchemizing
stone and dirt to lava and flesh. They are discharging.

Turning Around

I walk so fast through the apocalypse, skyscrapers
wake in front of me. One bows so low, I grab its antennae
and sing into it. It hurls me like a catapult to the world's edge.
There's only salt here and a pile of blisters. There is no end
or horizon to the beyond, but for a pair of shoulders.

Moving Image

The long hall is lined with television sets —
from spirals of apertures to detached picture tubes
to extended plasma screens with remotes — at the end,
a father is buried in a large maple veneer tv cabinet.
I feel almost nothing except for disinterestedness.

Medium Fairy Tale

I've been here before when there were more mountains.
I would pluck and stitch them to my chin. When the moon was
full, I'd cut them loose. They're now an asteroid belt.
The moon is not anymore a mirror, but, when full,
a palimpsest of my face inscribed with hardened lava pools.

Play: Atlas of Pleasure

In the first act, she lowers her eyes. In the second,
she's deep in the woods. She bites her nails and spits
them every hundred paces. In the third act, she whispers *help,*
a word she learned for God. In the fourth and fifth, when she's lost,
her fingers stray and she forgets her lines.

Troubadour and Toreador

She unzips her long red dress, steps from it, kicks the dress
up to a cape and taunts the bull. The bull charges. She leaps
and twists over its head and stabs it in the back with her stiletto
heels and breaks the neck with its horns. High in the corner
of the stadium, a poet with a stubby pencil takes notes.

City of Trams

A thousand naked ladies pace the Parthenon
with silk twisted through their hair. A cable car pulls up.
A man in a three-piece suit steps off, drops iron pennies
in the fountain, extends his paint brush, and approaches.
Women seated on the balconies fan themselves with shackles.

Untitled (Snail with Turtle)

At the garden's edge, a snail slides a sticky trail.
A turtle makes wakes through long grass. It will take days
before one yields their path and begs a pardon.
Meanwhile, the snail rolls a pair of dice for fate
to engender its sex, and the turtle turns inward.

Backyard Help

The neighborhood pond is blue as a tailed monster's eye.
When I strip, the houses turn away. My penis
is a rudder as I swim in circles, then drift
to the waterfall's pool, walled in with polished-off rocks.
The pond fills with cattails and gathers spies on all sides.

In Moon's Mud Time

I'm naked, again, of course, but I am not running away —
there's rain and no one sees me or I them. I can stand
in the waterfall's pond and spit and sing until it dries
into this lunar field. There's the shack, where I write and hide,
rising a little more each time it rains. It's only half under.

Ringing

After the apocalypse, it snows. Survivors wear wool coats
and walk dogs. Gray buildings congregate and language fractures
over crackling radios. The lunch lines are long. I remember
my high school locker combination, and my first girlfriend
is here. She says *yes,* but I can't stop thinking *last bell.*

Last Call

As she tells me how her husband's mother insists she's not
to leave the bedroom after dark, she lifts her left leg
along the barroom table, I stroke her green sock and listen,
she points it out, I drop my hand, I apologize.
We're in the parking lot after hours walking away.

Black Hole with Red and White Checkered Tablecloth

I light my pipe. She serves a plate of potatoes.
She's laid out a bowl of milk, a cup of coffee, a basket
of tangerines, a platter with a donut. A tangerine pops
into its hole, another, a stream of coffee, milk, potatoes, the smoke,
    then me
falling. My farewell stare — she's folding closed the tablecloth.

Hallway

At the end of the hallway is a crack.
With this step past the stairs, the crack is a door
blossoming into orange poppy. When I reach to pluck
a petal, the end of the hallway is a mirror
with someone tugging my hand from behind.

Night Tremor

I'm reading back cover book blurbs when rain arrives.
When lightning and thunder fall, I lock the front door.
I re-cover my books. The dry morning wakes me.
I open the door. Thunder is tangled in a tree.
Lightning encourages it to jump into the light.

Turned Back

It's my last day of tinkering with clocks
and the angle of my car's rearview mirror. It's the last day
I'll untie my shoes and count the steps to my bedroom.
It is the last time I'll measure my life — my compass
having drawn the full arc from the day I arrived.

Empty Suit

This CEO reminds me of my daughter doodling
(though less responsible and loopy), but he won't spin his chair.
His office phone rings and delivers urgent information
as her play phone, though less charming and meaningful. I miss
    her.
Only a graveyard is filled with the irreplaceable.

Untitled (Hallway with Binding)

The hallway curves into a vanishing point.
On one side, the carved wooden rail. On the other,
the wall and bookshelf with the book that anticipates me.
It's soft and drapes in my hands. Each page reads
to a story's end. Every morning begins like this.

Lesson Plan: Teaching Terroir 1638 A.D.

The first time you're lost,
scoop a handful of earth.
Rub a smudge across your gums
and tongue. Pocket the clump.

Do this at each occurrence.
When you're home, redistribute
the dirt along your kitchen
table in regions like a king.

Where you were lost,
press your thumb and spittle
drool into the hole.
Here, you'll grow your grapes.

And while you cannot mold time,
though it can age, nor plot
experience, you can name
your garden, and water and twist the vines.

When you bottle vinegar and wine
and offer it out for trade,
customers will learn your land
by tasting where you found your way.

1439 A.D. — This Is How the Middle Ages End

The last ship has docked,
the captain kicks the compass,
and the first mate rubs straw
over loadstone. They are safe

and lost with no measurable true
north. It's no longer a question
of delivering cinnamon and dye
to merchants or stories to harlots

and bankers in lieu of credit
and debt. There's the continual
explosion of a supernova —
a long star arc through the zodiac.

It will not give up its assertion —
light moves quicker than the word.
Somewhere in the deepest library,
a copyist begins retranslating
the last straight inch of history.

II

The Museum of Cartography

Medieval Cartographer's Prayer

I have seen the bright patterns that transmit
a message without a tongue. It shouts no words.
The pattern says, "Deliver me. Return me home."
May everyone understand the mystery of these lines.

Drought Season (Eurus Winds)

When the sun rises seven mornings in a row,
the eighth will deliver hot winds and empty night skies.
Newborns will wheeze through puffed, ruddy cheeks and swollen
    eyes.
Mothers will have to milk the land. You'll need white limning.

Early Islamic Stellar Cartography: Advanced Mediation

To sit upon an astrolabe and wait for God to intervene
or for the Devil to ascend from below and enter
into one's nether lands is the way of ventriloquists,
for us, it is to transcribe the sky on parchment or a napkin.

The Climate of Hell

Winter arrives from the north, an immigrant
wind with devil wings. It freezes our hair, burns
our faces, delivers us contradictions —
we are coldest when we're closest to the sun.

Dante's Map

Like most maps from the Middle Ages,
The *Inferno*'s a speculative map — sketched
hope and allegory. It forsakes the accurate.
It won't even help in forgiving our sins.

Typhoon Season (Zephyrus Winds)

Typhoons always rise from the west in summer
before the harvest when children learn to sing
from swans. When the last sea anemone flies by,
assess crop profits — color the land red or black.

Letter from Giovanni Francesco Camocio to Paulo Forlani, April,
    27, 1565

The whiteness of the page is your anxiousness —
it's the land you do not know. Since it's not yet yours,
leave it unbound. Plant tufts of crops, score odd beasts,
do what you will with this new world until I arrive.

Blasphemous Mapmaking Advice from the Middle Ages

Every map must encode a secret — hidden
treasure, a portal to hell, or proof the world
is a sphere — and its key decodes on the day
the sun casts no shadow and Cancer rises.

Lost Letter from Beatrice to Dante, May 7, 1290

Do not read or decipher
from the cartographer's map —
they will fill you with false hopes,
with visions from their own minds.

Lost Letter from Beatrice to Dante, May 11, 1290

When you send me uninvited cantos,
whose lines cut like paths through your version of hell,
I know you have no soul, for the soul, like God, speaks —
the devil is the one who writes the contracts.

Vellum Riddle

A knife removed all matters of dross.
Unable to speak, I could not say *no.*
Hundreds of black parallels marked on my back
illuminate the world. I tell you where you are.

In Plague Times (Auster Winds)

The country moves with the southern wind. If a lake
lies to the south, the wind draws frogs and grasshoppers
from the water. You must rest your pen and strain egg
whites on your map. When the world dries, scrape and revise.

Antony Knivet's Notes on Simian Life in the Southern
  New World 1592

The howling monkeys do not eat or drink. They live
off the air and roar like a thousand tortured zebras.
The map I draw has no scythe or bones — Death
treads water off the coast of Chile with wax in his ears.

Ice Storms (Boreas Winds)

When the forest sags like melted wax,
go to the printing room and cover
the plates with dung and straw. The world's second
edition will thaw similar enough.

Jacob's Cross

Hold it like Captain Ahab would steady a rifle
aiming to shoot down the sun. If you lack confidence,
your sighting eye will go blind like every atheist
who's sailing lost below the equator and cursing.

A Lizard Log

Since the moon changed, we have seen neither horizon
nor sun and have scarce a thing to burn. The alarm
clock rings each hour — reminding me of my gout.
We have entered an immeasurable ocean.

Then from the Deck

The crew hands released the ropes. Were we looking up to them,
we'd have felt the hurriedness of abandonment, the quick
scaling of size. Looking down instead, we fostered our sense
of scale. Our raft cut the sea, and we felt something colder.

Dead Reckoning

We realigned the shock absorbers on the oars and keel.
We tied fishing line to the chronometers and flew them
like weather balloons through Jupiter's lunar eclipses.
still the parallels form no better than dead reckoning.

Medieval Stellar Cartography

Any planets or moons that enter your head or belly
or anywhere and form in your mouth as words are divine,
but should you write or draw from where they came, you will
    deceive
heaven and find deafness in music of the spheres and your head.

Man Overboard

Eventually, when you're sinking and you've lost
hold of the rope, sunlight stops. You realize
you've never seen black before, or violence.
It's too late to change course, and bubbles chart your fall.

Rough Drafts

Some maps get lost and disintegrate into the earth.
Other maps blow overboard and sink. All treasure maps
are stolen, memorized, and eaten. A few maps survive.
I once burned everything I wrote, and left my mark.

The Cartographer's Credo

You can always go more
and more west. The sun
never stops, even when
it's under the earth.

Or if you're a channeler
of night skies, black holes
will appear like purple gyre
spumes. You just have to focus,

or reimagine the limits
of light speed, how you walk
through time, or how you'll sail
your ship across the ripples of space.

Like a man thrown overboard
whose dying body pulls
his shadow down with him,
you must commit.

The Cartographer's Advice

Only so much can be realized
with black inscription on parchment —
the houses, the roads, the palaces.
Your map may even lead the hurried princes
and tithe collectors where they need to go.
When your country becomes predictable
to draw, materially dull, depict bodies
of water as cultivated fields or untaxed farms.
Your map is nothing more than a land
bible filled with symbols
to be interpreted when lost.
Sometimes a country needs rediscovery.

The Unmentionable Places for the Cartographer

The edge of the world can be seen
leaving her hand. There's no atlas
or formally attired elephants, here.
Obviously, nothing can stand
in a swamp where light and stars fall —
it's darker than before a dream.

And there are many swamps on the periphery —
some evolve into the long futures
of oil and stock exchanges,
some are shoe factories, some a field
in southern Mississippi with a white barn
and hanging tree, some the Pentagon —
you know, all the places you cover your eyes from
and they write commandments about.

When her hand returns, she draws Victoria Falls,
washes her hands, and regrets what next she will draw.

The Treasure Gaze as Explained by Abraham Cresques Using His Catalan Atlas

The tourist steadies this map to study
its nodes. He tries to trace the spray of lines
as paths. He views the world from upside down
and clockwise round. He'll swoon in dizziness.
But you, who have caressed a foreign lace
and washed in porcelain tubs with perfumed soaps,
move patiently with stares from flag to flag.
You search for gold and turquoise I inlaid.
At times, I sense you're feigned disinterest,
your plottings to appropriate this map
without acknowledging what I have drawn,
like god recording treasures from the sky.
Like god, I know your thrills. They're not for you —
Cease your gaze. Read the map's legend for me.

Finding North

The first mapmakers were anonymous,
but we can know the time and place they drew
by studying symbols of scale and space.
Before Italians recognized their land
as boot, they drew the winds as lines across
the Mediterranean Sea, and drew
the compass rose to point to where they blew.
The Catalans invested first to sketch
the coast then lines to navigate from port
to port. To mark directions, they composed
the compass chicken — its beak points true north.
And now we know the Turks first rolled the earth
into a ball and tied a bow of rhumb lines to the top.

The First Line of Prayer

The first line, as it is told,
extended from me to you,
from her to him. It zigzagged
and twisted through town.
It touched everyone,
including the ungulates and cows.
It rooted trails and roads to houses.

The line rose slowly and thickened
into a wall. The Great Wall
of China formed this way.
You can still walk atop its road
in two discrete directions.
You can see it from space,
if you're a god.

And in this way, houses rose
into churches. The loftier
the church, the more prevailing view.
If you sang from here,
the ungulates perked their tails.
With the lower church songs,
the cows laid down on all fours.

If you don't know today where you are,
you won't know how to sing
Your god — your mediation
to your place in the world —
is the origin point, if you plot it,
to your yet extended line.
May it stay grounded, tangled, flat.

Transcendental Homelessness

There are noseless men
fishing in the Red Sea.

Their tongues are bruised
and their flesh flakes.

When the snow falls,
they think it's from them.

If spring comes to them,
they hope to sprout leaves.

As the sea freezes, they dream
of flat fish and salted bread.

They dream their decaying bodies
will have a transcendent perfume.

Artic Circle Cautioning (352 B.C.)

If you travel north with urgency
past the last measurement
and through the speculations,

if you see atmosphere
non-distinct from geology
and ocean surface,

if you feel gelatinous,
shut quick your mouth
before it jumps and scurries off,

put your ear to the borealis,
curl your fingers into canoes,
hold your breath, and burrow.

The North will melt. You will float
home — the home pockmarked by salt
and pressure from a deepening sea.

The Vertical Moment

When he could not measure,
he would weave
with a slide rule,
dashing as a shuttle.

With three-hundred-sixty
woolen hemispheres,
he was wrapped up
in looming new worlds.

We unmade our beds
and slept on their corners.
We dreamed longitudes
and woke to latitudes.

In the morning,
he turned us
to where the sun first rose
then where the moon last set.

He showed us the curve
to east-west
and the gentle bending
away of stars.

Johannes Deville, the First Atheist Cartographer

He favored content over destination.
If a child played hoops in the street,
he mimicked her minutest detail.

He drew her with dots and the country,
the houses and taverns, the ponds
and goldfish. He drew with black

on white vellum. He drew the calf
that gave its skin to this land.
He plotted battlefields and graveyards.

Even the wind took hold with powdered silver
scattered from west to east.
He despised cherubs beyond the borders.

He believed in grounding observation.
He's in every map below the legend —
that tiny shadow holding a pen.

The World from a Genoese

In 1457, there is his eye-
shaped world, a map, a catalog of beasts
and fish. A dragon and cargo ships off coasts.
A giraffe in Africa spots them.
It sees everything before the mapmaker
begins to think to sketch new territories
or a slave at center earth like the small hand
of a clock at three in the afternoon.
In all the world there's only one sea
for commerce. The whole world is
the mapmaker's astigmatism. It's very dry.
If he blinks, we'll be washed out and Africa
will never trade with anyone on earth.

The White Space

As noted before,
you draw a map by ear.
You listen to the land,

children crying,
the ignition of canons,
your instincts

of where the moral belong —
the painters, the bakers,
the weavers, the farmers,

the ones who create,
the ones who use their hands —
which is everywhere.

For the others —
the bankers, the princes,
those with scented hands —

you're inclined to give them space
off the world map
or at the bottom of a sea —

any place without sound.
This inclination is not sound,
or rather it is

the idea for sheet music —
its arrangement of notation
on a musical map —

the staff, the treble clef,
the sharps and flats,
eighth notes, and allegros.

Your inclination will chart
a breezy composition for the handy ones
and score the rest in blank tablature.

Martin Behaim to Pope Clement VI on the Incomplete Maps (1342 A.D.)

No two countries are the same,
and before Easter arrives,
their boundaries will shift,
again, from war or politics
or the slip of a copyist's pen.

Or will be found a new animal,
or a race of people will be acknowledged,
these maps will read like stories.
Or someone will invent a cross-staff,
a compass, or a nocturnal.
Or the discovery of precious mineral
or spice will inspire accuracy
in the maps you desire.

Where does that land end?

Does the sea surround the world?

I cannot know. The Pole Star
wanders like a guard
looking for a place to nap.
Sometimes it settles out of sight,
and I pray the Little Dipper
to not disappear and for Spain
to be where it was
and always should be.

You can play your trumpet and hope
angels echo you home, but often
there is no horizon or boundary
to discover. The world spins too fast
to be transcribed.

The Mapmaker's Pleasure Principle (1488 A.D.)

If on your travels
you relocate a city
closer to home

just because
you like its taverns
and pretty women,

leave a memorial
to mark your stay,

but if you push
a city away
just because

you don't want
to carry everywhere
the alley with nameless children,

the church with unstained glass,
the bakery with stale bread,
the calloused memories you built,

erect at the city limits
a marker for what
you walked away from.

Scale your distances
in inclinations.

Hic Sunt Vaccas

From here we walk a mile down this road.
Before their war, the path was cobblestone,
but now, packed rubble. Though the wall remains.
It cuts our field in half. That side grows wheat.
In fall, the husks spike red, and pests arrive.
Something's always arriving — the lightning,
the humid winds, the armies with their guns.
A Tiger tank's tracks snapped off in that field.
Sometimes the things that come retreat, like light
of day, like onslaught of death, like their war.
And here is where I was born, as noted
on this plaque beside our memorial.
If you move here, you will learn to not forget.
And here are those cows you came to skin.

Drawing to Scale (900 A.D.)

When determining distance
between yours and theirs,
don't rely on merchants.

Their world is larger
and more valuable —
fish became armor,

slaves were hairy giants,
purple dye was stolen
from slaughtered dragons,

and wool sheared by Cyclopes.
You can measure a shadow
or calculate the height

of star if you want,
but on cloudy days
or when lacking measures,

trust your senses —
the windiest places
are nearest oceans and seas,

the most populated lands
are the most important
and therefore the biggest,

if you think mountains
exist, sketch in a range
of binding treaties with spines —

draw the world flat
so boundaries and conflicts
may fold over.

Guide to Medieval Reading

A book in buckled clasps will need a key.
Save those for last. If bound in thongs or wrapped
in belts, then you may open those. But first,
lower your head. With your left hand, hold the spine
and lift it lightly from the shelf. Then turn
the pages with your right. Skim before you read.
If the book is new, you'll smell the printer's hands
and spits of ink, especially the reds.
Don't read it here. Find a quiet corner,
to better sense the tricks of tongue and teeth.
The words might jettison quick, and you'll lose
their meanings. Read slow. Listen with intent.
But first convince the Curator to have you.
Be blessed before you touch the books.

III

Exile on Longleaf Trace

Wisteria

If you ever remove your orange velvet skirt,
I will write clockwise songs down your back
and counterclockwise notations
of euphony up your thighs —
but only if you gesture the *yes* to be entwined.

Crabapple

I was first attracted to your stretch marks —
shepherd's crook scars like gray rainbows
curled around each hip — complements
to your mottled inner thighs —
procreation and death from the wild hind.

Yaupon

Three uninspired moments of inspiration:
your hips sliding into my jeans,
Sartre's *Nausea* on the bar's sawdust floor,
you secretly whispering in my ear —
drink this black.

Tulip Poplar

Each April, I hear words of your arrival.
Sometimes in French, other times Celtic,
though never my language of conjuring.
Each time I hear your mistranslated name —
a little deeper settles your spell.

Shortleaf Pine

These are the letters you said you read
but did not because I had not
yet written them down or sent them out —
these are all the words in our world
that fell and settled like seeds.

Blackgum

Our pillows are stuffed with feathers
from quails, our mattress from partridges —
the remains from a steady stream of meals
to support us for as long as we fuck —
until the river sinks our bed.

Supplejack

Our first glass of red wine
soothes our smoke-scratched throats
as it settles down counterclockwise.
I feel susceptible like a caged peacock —
your hand gathers what it's brought forth.

Chinese Tallow Tree

That first time you drew a bath
and folded my pants and the years
following when you wrote letters
with purple dye, you were like common rice —
something most useful to me and stickier.

Bamboo

During dinner, you presented well my food
and drink. At last call, you ornamented me well
and cured my impotence, if only briefly.
You were so versatile and enduring —
now a memory hobbled with splints.

Eastern Dogwood

"This is the twin bed we slept on
for years. Here is our new king bed."
"You won't be able to find me."
"You will need to amplify my dreams." —
"I will bake you each night a narcotic cake."

Sparkleberry

The first night we didn't make love, your eyes,
the dull hue of blackbird eggs,
shook with every heartbeat.
When we returned to the wild and needed courage —
I gave you the lungs and liver of a doe.

Groundsel

When I awake, you will have pinched me
black and blue, and I'll ask for the door.
If instead I give to you a gift tonight —
this lock — will you untwist your fingers —
crack them in the hinges?

Loblolly Pine

When I read the first page
in your herbaceously bound book,
I find copyright and colophon,
then the accretion of poems —
an inflorescence of meaningless rush.

Southern Magnolia

You have never been to Mississippi
except by email. You count happiness
like buckshot wounds. You skip
through every puddle like a scalpel through oil —
I'm a Tiger tank spinning in muddy replies.

Sandalwood

After you email me, I need a shot
of whiskey and a long walk
to where the hieroglyphs grow —
where grass and sidewalk verge —
walking back does not translate to reply.

Sweetgum

My dear, wild pears ripen very slowly
even when drizzled with honey.
Take this slice of dry apple in the while.
You'll like it just as fine —
it ripened in the ice age and was stolen from a swine.

Elliott's Blueberry

When you fly and your ears cramp,
it means you have a secret you don't want
to share. Chew on this parsley
for courage. It blossomed up a chimney —
from a pot of butter and dung.

Beautyberry

You have arranged your dolls
on the dining room table and bound them
with rice straw. You serve them wine like adults
and tell them how a baby is made —
limbs and body stitched from skin of fallen cranes.

Wax Myrtle

You have been carrying a stolen testicle
since we met. You turn it in your pocket.
On the gulf's shore, as salt and rain settle
in your hair, you layer kelp across my thighs —
I sink in the sand broken, wormy, punky.

Lilac

It's time for me to love you again —
here is our bed and here are our tourniquets.
Tie one to each pinewood post.
I will write you a letter about oranges,
I hope you will flute a bluish song.

Sassafras

When I step away from the library of trees,
the sky is flat and long, meandering.
I smell words like *first* and *last*.
You can consider this a reply —
an ungerminated seed.

Longleaf Pine

If you boil my letters, a yellow dye yields.
Paint with it. If you burn them,
like salt they will flame orange. Cook with it.
If you cut them, weave the shreds into clothes —
do whatever is essential or do not reply.

Scripture

I learned to write watching mother
mow the lawn. Back and forth. Ruling
perfect lanes that her thin shadow marked.
She did this every week — cutting and marking.

Inscribing Myself

There is
a rack of skin

in place and time
thinking like you

from left to right
and down and down

the sound of your mind
moving if it speaks

if it will abstract
sounds from words

the pencil
scratching paper

each poem is all the residue
from that whole pencil

the nervous itch
you feel at every line's end

Deconstruction

He handed me my college diploma.
My arm yellowed and stiffened with six sides.
My arm an unsharpened pencil with cuffs,
a hand, and a sheet of authorized paper.
He congratulated my graduation,
patted me on the shoulder, and pointed me
off stage. I swung my arm to shake it loose
and knocked a chair into the hardwood floor.
It splattered *c, h, a, i,* and *r.*
I hugged my mother into *m, o,* and *m.*
Then my left hand dripped *f, i, n, g, e, r, s,*
h, a, n, and *d* into a puddle.
My world decomposed without my intent.
I touched myself and dissolved into *e, g,* and *o.*

Under the Spell of an Increasingly Deadly Vowel Movement

I did not show up today as I lost my E.
Forward, backward, and right I could try,
but only into a past without you.
So I did not show to that party,
now two months away from this May day,
and as I hastily go, soon April and stopping
in March, a month of mortality for I.
What can a body say among rot,
marrow, and loss? And now fatally lost, oh,
what an abysmally bad day and why?

The Orange Movement and the Rise and Fall of
Orange Nucléaire

The Orange Movement arrived in Luxemburg and Brazil independently, simultaneously, and in the final year of the war. In Luxemburg, the movement commenced at an art show with Oldenburg's *Orange Propositions,* and in Brazil with Barrow's dance performance *How to Explain Orange to a Gentoo Penguin.* Oldenburg's art arose from the Rococo and the Fauvists, whilst Barrow's arose from Geometric Abstractionism. Oldenburg's pigments were red and yellow, and Barrow danced with his feet bound together by orange ribbons. Both artists revolted. After the war, Pivotalist sculptor Tschirnhaus brought the two together in Antwerp at the *Orange Hour,* the first gathering of artists concerned with Space Age and the Atomic Era and who provided artistic resistance against the rising uses of technology. Gerhardt made an appearance with his musical number *My Position in the Battle Between the Threats of Seed and Pulp,* which confronted the issue of Ephemeralization in the modern age. At this one-time encounter, the four of them collaborated on the inter-medial art form *Orange Nucléaire.* This yoking together of painting, dancing, sculpture, and music was the first conscious endeavor where the media filled the unquantifiable and emotional space between the work and spectator. The effects were overwhelming as the spectators left vibrating with communal fusion for days. The irrational and imaginative space, the kinetic field of bond and flow, however, wholly evaporated at the showing's end, as did the spectators days later. With the middle space breached and with the art a remainder of object, the artists returned to their homes with a phosphorescent glow and conducted a long series of homages to evaporation and the end of orange.

Response

The challenge is to indicate where I have been.
I could point backward and say, "From there,"
but the voice is a poor instrument —
it can't erase, it can only speak louder.

I could write a story or draw a map,
either way, I'd make a long metaphor,
draw out some significant moments
and scratch out wherever I slept or pissed.

If you like watching through tinted windows,
my van could take us back on hard roads
and a series of pitstop associations —
we can remake a life together, or not.

Perhaps your question was simpler than all that.
It's been so long since we shared a space.
I hear between your words, but, more, I watch —
I want to invoke meaning in your presence.

Conversation on the Balcony

You're stiff as stripes.

Your hairs disappear into your robe
like displaced ducks.

> Are you a pencil or a pen?
> I want to click your head
> or erase with it.

Why do you float
duck heads in our ponds?

> To draw your hand
> from your pocket.

You mean unravel my stripes?

> I mean, it's bedtime.
> You're like a tree.

Your thighs are like my nightmares.

> I have an orange scarf
> across my breasts.

I shall pretend
it's autumn.

> Yes.

Gerard Mercator Dreams of the Rhumb Line

This was the first time
I was on this planet,
or was it an island?
No matter. The sun was the same.

The air she threw rocks
against trying to make rain
or snow or make a hole
to crawl through was flammable.

She hid there like in an oven
or a spaceship home.
She twisted and rolled
my maps into a fuse.

The last time here, I stack
the rocks and patch the holes —
the sun drifting across ashes
like the first day of fasting.

Sometimes the Night Arrives Without Design

I've seen it twice before. The first, one spring,
its sudden winds erased the daylit sky,
and reinscribed with cold and larkspur blue.
The second time occurred in middle June —
the sea's horizon ebbed instead of rose,
and merchant ships returning home sailed off
their maps. Trade winds sank and water dried to land.
Today I stare long into the east.
I hold my saxophone across the wind
and listen hard for changes in earth's pitch.
I have my armor and butterfly net.
The night will not surprise this time, I have
apologies to write and shadows to defend.

Sometimes I Contact My First Love at Night

To draw Pangea accurately,
not from the imagination of shoving
together apparent facts and coastlines,
one needs a time machine or very old pen.

A pen that old, however, can't be found
unless you have a time machine. Of course,
no such machine has appeared in our time,
which means even the future is lost.

Thus, you need to meditate to connect
to god. If you do, she will mediate
through you to any old pen you have
and push it to draw that desired contour.

I once had this straight, powerful line
of connection with her. My hand moved.
I touched the line. It fell. And leave it
to my dog to gnaw that spirit's power line.

I could not reconnect and finish
the coast just as I cannot create
a time machine or retrieve an ancient pen.
I don't know anymore why I try to write her.

Still the Bells

Each day the ground just looks the same. I turn
around and walk away the day, then sit,
untie my shoes, and listen to the bells,
except there is no church or tower near,
nor cat nor cow. It's morning dark. Just stars
and grass. But there are words and they draw lines
between the stars and count the blades of grass.
The constellations always seem incomplete
to me and *Leaves of Grass* a pointless prayer.
But still the bells and words. My toes are cold.
The sun is near and soon it will erase the night.
I don't know why I write you every day,
and wait till dark to send it in the mail,
when still the ground's the same, when still the bells.

Even Now

Even now, there is pollen
from the first sneeze. I've kept it
under glass with your eyelashes —
one day I'll blow it in your eyes.

Even now, my pockets are filled
with handkerchiefs and worms —
the birds wake me in the morning
and I wipe myself dry.

Even now, when I burn a beehive
your thighs come to mind,
and when I eat hot honey,
the roof of my mouth wrinkles.

Even now, the pile of bricks
have been stacked into a wall.
I hid one brick so there's a hole
where we can pass each other notes.

Even now, in winter, you bury a sardine
can with all your ideas and postage stamps.
"Art," you say, "requires no images.
It's purely mechanics, like a clock and a bomb."

Even now, there is no one like her —
her frenzied mouth and right arm throwing wine
glasses at my head. My timid soul would duck
if it weren't already razed on the kitchen floor.

Even now, as I wait for the aliens to land
or the bomb to drop, I learn new numbers
for counting time forwards and back,
but wherever I am, it's ground zero.

Even now, my long eyelashes
blink and spiders fall
from the ceiling. It's like flirting
before the invention of money.

Even now, you are geometry
with utilitarian meaning. Urge
and urge, the aesthetics of sex —
the quintessence of free will.

Even now, when I mix red wine
with oleander, I'll walk the streets,
dig a tall hole, plant a totem
of you, and spit up foam.

Even now, you're a ballerina
spinning in a mirror
like your orange skirt wrung out to dry
or your fingers in a prayer at last call.

Even now, I'm learning to fuck
in a poem. Spondee. Spondee.
Caesura. Stanza break. Who cares.
It's over. I like to metaphor you.

Even now, boot black and orange
are the colors of poverty
and the disinterested.
Your hair is their reins.

Even now, when you watch the puppet play
within the puppet play, you think
you're trapped or an unwashed sock
at the doorway to a laundromat.

Even now, you blame the mirror
for the flection of your face —
yes, it's crooked like crisis,
like debt, like the ledger of beauty.

Even now, my love is doomed
to make me a cuckold, like betrayed
Russian revolutionaries. It's what I want.
Sex and self-sustenance are so tiring.

Even now, the Longleaf Trace is shady
and dusty like your favorite book
you've read through a hundred times — you've become
accustomed to blisters and turn the page.

Even now, you carry notebooks and step
across cracked pathway stones.
Not breaking any backs, you're a hero,
and a martyr for any word you misspell.

Even now, spilled wine
is like forgetting a book.
I can inscribe you again,
if you can clutch a corkscrew.

Even now, the portrait I painted
of you, the feet and ankles,
the thighs, and the hips,
is all I need to remember of you.

Even now, your nose punctures
your face, your eyes draw
in light, your lips suck atmosphere —
you cut into space with little matter.

Even now, egg cowries wash ashore.
They'll return to sea like birds,
to farms where the scarecrow blows over,
or to me in a canoe with a butterfly net.

Even now, my collection of holes,
which blossomed grass and dandelions
and flooded with black water,
are labelled with tombstones.

Even now, the sun rises,
a baby dies before it's born,
a grandmother reasons with dream logic,
and there are dirty dishes to scrub and stairs to count.

Even now, when I have breakfast
in the nook and the orange sun rises
behind me, I read the news and bite a peach
like it will answer universal questions.

Even now, if I could see her again
like a movie in an empty theater,
the floor would be sticky
and I'd be asked to leave.

Even now, I've learned to write
in the X and Y dimensions — utopian
and proletarian idealisms — I have learned
to write the historical gaps of Z.

Even now, when I fuck against a mirror,
the refraction of sex has a social side — utilitarian
invention — our lovemaking, however worded,
was like filing paperwork after hours.

Even now, I can still hear you complain,
"I'm still so cold." The frozen worm
I fed you hasn't yet thawed.
When it does, you will protest the warmth.

Even now, I see your face in water
at the bottom of a pothole,
in the toilet before I sit,
flowing through the hole in my canoe.

Even now, the stage curtain, the footlights,
the proscenium arch are attacks
on the lyric mode — on stage,
which is everywhere, you are drama.

Even now, as I plant orchids in gunpowder,
light a match, look to my watch
and countdown, I notice you
still have a time for a final smell.

Even now, each revolution, I mean, affair,
is an historical instance to rename
opportunity, I mean, who's on top —
the aura from a theatrical relationship.

Even now, the image is subject
or the subject is abstraction or sound,
even a post-it note can stand in,
you, you, you are an object for you.

Even now, each month I receive a note
from the usurers bearing interest
from your carefree love. The smaller
I make the debt, the less I remember you.

Even now, (hands on the city clock) (time)
in Oneonta (counterclockwise
maddening), (clockwise devised)
a madman lives in the future.

Even now, the blackbird sings
in the orange tree. If our bruises
could sing, but they can't. So grab
my ass and fuck me til I scream.

Even now, love does not flow
from the poem. It cannot
delight in itself :: fog on a stream,
children's play in the evening haze.

Even now, the geese fly in an inverted V —
the way your feet spread from years of suffering
ballet or a trap a wolf gnaws free its paw —
no, rather, in fact, it is a less-than symbol.

Even now, when I dry seaweed
to use for your statue's hair,
the salt eats away the face —
you appear as a mask.

Even now, in the periphery,
lampposts walk into southern magnolia shade.
If the telephone poles follow,
I'll send you smoked signals.

Even now, I don't mourn the loss
of money I invested in you,
I mean, in sustaining your privileges —
I design inexpensive poems for non-consumers.

Even now, a river runs
down the middle of your bed —
a river runs through you —
a river runs through a good cry.

Even now, the fifteenth anniversary
of the bonfire where I read all my poems —
spoken once then floated to ash —
I rewrite on a hard drive.

Even now, the Longleaf Trace is moving
like my favorite tune
I've sung a hundred times —
even with blisters, I walk miles to sing.

Even now, her lock of hair
is tied to the bed post.
I stroke it before I sleep
and dream of temple doors.

Even now, when I go to sleep
my eyelashes are ribs
around nightmares and forgetting.
In the morning, you spread them.

Even now, after all the bookcases and bookshelves
and all that reading before they were stacked,
I have not yet learned to properly read
a goodbye, a tombstone, or "addressee has moved."

Even now, the bed sags in the middle
and smells of twenty-five years.
I'd much rather sleep now or tomorrow,
than tour another of our rivers.

Notes

The "Night Tremor" section of "Dream Atlas" is after Alexander Long, and the "Empty Suit" section of "Dream Atlas" is for Sophie.

"The Chorographer's Advice" — The chorographer's "concern is to paint a true likeness, and not merely to give exact positions and size . . . and no one gets it rightly unless he is an artist." — Ptolemy.

"Transcendental Homelessness" is a term from Georg Lukacs. It means something like the longing for a place where one once belonged as well as the "nostalgia . . . for utopian perfection." In a godless world, an emptiness is left behind for which the soul can find no place to exist.

A "Jacob's Cross" (in "The Museum of Cartography") is a tool used to measure the height of the sun to determine latitude.

"Hic Sunt Vaccas" translated from Latin to English is "Here Are Cows."

"Even Now" is after Hugo Claus's "Even Now."

The line "a river runs through a good cry" in "Even Now" comes from the writings of Rebecca Mae Holder.

River — A large stream of water. Also, "a term for the sag furrowed in a mattress by love-making" (Robert Graves in *The White Goddess*).

The characters in the poems are either fictitious (such as Johannes Deville) or once lived (such as Dante and Beatrice). For those that once lived, their events depicted in the poems are fictitious.

Dedications

"In Bas-Relief" is for Anna Beth Rowe.

"Dedication from *Love's Apostrophe,* an Anonymous Book of Love Poems from 1082 A. D." is for Wanda Schubmehl.

"The Treasure Gaze as Explained by Abraham Cresques Using His Catalan Atlas" is for Bryana Fern.

"Finding North" is for Paul Allen.

"Hic Sunt Vaccas" is for Jennifer Bozzette.

"Guide to Medieval Reading" is for Maryam Ala Amjadi.

"Sometimes the Night Arrives Without Design" is for Ruth Foley.

"Sometimes I Contact My First Love Late at Night" is for Garrett Ashley.

Special thanks to Rob Carney, Thomas Alan Holmes, and Rebecca Mae Holder for early readings, Dr. Craig Carey (who unknowingly is the inspiration/impetus for this collection), Dr. Charles Sumner, Dr. Martina Sciolino, Dr. Angela Ball, Dr. Rebecca Morgan Frank, and, of course, Max Macpherson.

About the Author

Tom Holmes is the editor of *Redactions: Poetry & Poetics* and the author of four full-length collections of poetry, including *Material Matters* and *The Cave* (winner of The Bitter Oleander Press Library of Poetry Book Award for 2013), as well as four chapbooks. He teaches at Nashville State Community College, Clarksville. His writings about wine, poetry book reviews, and poetry can be found at his blog: *The Line Break*: *thelinebreak.wordpress.com/*. Twitter: @TheLineBreak

www.ingramcontent.com/pod-product-compliance
Lightning Source LLC
Chambersburg PA
CBHW022015080426
42733CB00007B/612